Daybreak and Deep

Daybreak and Deep

Poems by

Jessica D. Thompson

Jessica D. Thompson

Cover design by Shay Culligan
Cover art by Catrin Welz-Stein

ISBN: 978-1-63980-155-8

Kelsay Books
502 South 1040 East, A-119
American Fork, Utah 84003
Kelsaybooks.com

For my sisters: Pat and Eva

Acknowledgments

The author wishes to thank the following journals which first gave her poems a home, sometimes in earlier forms:

Atlanta Review: "Upon the Death of a Poet"

Barnwood: "Parting the Crows"

Bloodroot: "Made Beautiful," "Sunday"

Bullets and Blank Bibles (a Chapbook from Liquid Paper Press): "A Morning in Spring," "After the Service," "Bare Feet and Long Night Gowns," "Boy Kings," "Future Home of the Mammoth Mega Church," "How to Grieve in Winter," "Inkblot (Married Sleep)," "Parting the Crows," "Solitude Flats," "The Beekeeper's Daughter," "The Mourners," "The Reckoning," "The Shooters," "To the Girl in the Class Photo," "What Holds Us Up," "Wild Violets"

Chaffin Journal: "The Reckoning"

forty-one south: "Solitude Flats"

Kansas City Voices: "Tall Grass"

Mapping the Muse a Bicentennial Look at Indiana Poetry (Brick Street Poetry): "Praise Be to Crows"

Midwest Quarterly: "Killing Time"

Nerve Cowboy: "Boy Kings," "Still Life After Abstinence," "To the Girl in the Class Photo"

New Southerner: "The Blacksmith," "The Naming"

Next Indiana Campfires: a Trail Companion (Indiana Humanities): "Future Home of the Mammoth Mega Church"

Not Like the Rest of Us an Anthology of Contemporary Indiana Writers: "This God of My Waking"

Pegasus (the Prize Poems issue of the Kentucky State Poetry Society): "The Beekeeper's Daughter"

Plain Spoke: "Something So Grand"

Public Pool: "Adrift," "The Blue Light of May"

Ruminate Magazine: "This God of My Waking"

Sow's Ear Poetry Review: "Inkblot (Married Sleep)"

Still: The Journal: "The Mood Ring Diaries," "Sitting with the Dead"

The Heartland Review: "Daybreak and Deep," "The Mourners," "What Holds Us Up"

The Southern Review: "Worn"

Tiferet Journal: "Where the Crocus Waits"

Tipton Poetry Journal: "Future Home of the Mammoth Mega Church"

Women Speak, Vol. 7 (Women of Appalachia Project, Sheila-Na-Gig Editions): "The Blacksmith"

Thank you to my husband, Phil,
who inspires and shares my writing life.

With special thanks to Tom Raithel, Linda Neal Reising,
and Mark Williams, my *First Mondays Writers* family,
who were the first to read many of the poems in this collection.

…and…

In Memoriam

Hugh T. Thompson, Jr. (1950 – 2015)

Contents

Foreword

Jessica D. Thompson lives at the edge of a forest in Southern Indiana. Nearby is *The Roofless Church,* a "house of prayer for all people," a parabola dome with sculpted waves for walls, the push and pull of days. It is a place that, when I stand in it and look up beyond those walls and through the dome's open eye, I am drawn into a soft, surrounding silence. I feel nearer to what was once called heaven, even as my feet are very much on this earthen ground.

In *Daybreak and Deep,* Thompson gives us another roofless church: a collection of poems so delicately tuned to the ecology of love and loss that the book itself is indeed a house of prayer for all people, for all creatures, for every leaf and bloom and weed, for this heartbreak, heaven of a life.

—Rebecca Gayle Howell,
Author of *American Purgatory* and *Render/An Apocalypse*
and Poetry Editor, Oxford American

The breeze at dawn has secrets to tell you.

Don't fall back to sleep.

—Rumi

I

Waking

Daybreak and Deep

where pines are but a dark blur,
the barred owls

are at it again—declaring God-
knows-what,

past the gone-
to-weeds garden.

I sit facing east
before making the bed.

The scent of my pillow
like sunlight and old books.

The shape of my head
still visible there.

The same happenstance way
that tall grass

lays
after deer abandon sleep.

Overnight, the trees
dropped

their pine cones.
This morning,

I pulled more strands of hair
from my brush.

It happens every year—
school buses

bumping down the road,
the slowing churn of crickets,

arrival of crows in corn stubble.
The sound of leaves

trembling—
like tambourines in trees.

Bare Feet and Long Night Gowns

At five, I pulled my
reluctant four-year old brother

to the front of the one room
church where we sang

at the top of our lungs,
He's got the whole world

in His hands.
Before sleep, beneath

the Big Dipper, I twirled
in long night gowns—

spinning round and round
until I ran out of breath,

until the earth caught fire
beneath my bare feet,

and I fell—trusting,
onto the electric grass.

This God of My Waking

I still had my milk teeth
when I saw him drop

to his knees in the dark
Appalachian dirt,

the serpent severed in half.
Mother running, tearing

at the strings of her apron,
tendrils of hair

escaping her bun. Wild
pink and white morning

glories
reaching for light.

She saved him with words
she gave to the wind.

She saved him when
she took fire into her mouth.

Three times she went there.
Three times she spat.

Only then did I dare believe
he was mortal—

this god of my waking
days

falling to earth.

The Blacksmith

Before a hammer meets an anvil,
there is a pause midair

and time is suspended.
He forged horseshoes in a fire

built each day before sunrise.
Before bed, he would brush

her hair one hundred strokes.
I never saw such tenderness.

He must have thought of water
falling from a sun-struck cliff.

He must have thought of rose
petals floating in a rain barrel.

He must have thought he heard
a whisper of wings—

a sparrow
singing in the palm of his hand.

To the Girl in the Class Photo
Second Row, Third from the Left

I have heard the summer dust crying to be born
                    —Robinson Jeffers

We chased dust devils on the playground,
prayed they would pick us up,

carry us to another land—
like in the *Wizard of Oz*.

In the third grade, while standing
next to me in the auditorium,

you fainted from hunger
and were carried away

in the swirl
of a hand-me-down dress.

That was the last time anyone saw you.
Soon after,

they took your father's shotgun
house for the Sherman Minton Bridge.

The Mood Ring Diaries

We lived in a time of iron lungs and Marlboro
men, where feral dogs with matted eyes

and rock-hard balls
ruled the streets of our childhood,

and rats multiplied in alleys
behind matchbox houses, and friends

spent a year in bed with rheumatic fever,
and the dust of summer stayed all year—

it lifted like prayers
from the footfalls of barefoot children,

and some of us would die young
from eating flecks of lead-based paint

picked like flower petals from plastered
walls. It tasted like cabbage roses

in faded wallpaper. It tasted like communion
wafers, and we were taught to sit up straight,

to smile—to be seen, but never heard.
Years later, we wore mood rings

to regulate our feelings,
and while our brothers ran off to war,

we ran to altars
where bridesmaids stood like saints

in dotted Swiss dresses.
We wore the white of the sacrificed,

tied the knot,
spent the rest of our lives

keeping everything inside
prized, knotty pine cabinets.

Wild Violets

A woman in a faded dress
takes my quarter for a vase

I don't really need. I tell her
it looks like rain. Something

to break the silence.
Another family farm is sold.

Soon these wheat fields
will be covered in concrete.

Beyond the barn, an old man
walks between the rows.

There are no plastic flowers
there. No floral wreaths

beneath the sky.
Only wild violets grow

beside the standing stones.

The Shooters

Outside the shell of a mobile home,
men come to shoot guns,

their jaws loaded with tobacco,
they spit in the place where peace

roses once bloomed.
Now handmade signs advertise,

Spot Shoot Every Sunday.
When it gets cold, the men

stand around a wood stove,
smoke curling around their boots

like cats
who have grown too old to hunt.

Future Home of the Mammoth Mega Church

This land has been a working farm
for as long as I can remember.

Come late fall, the song of frogs
and their, *Hurry! Hurry!*

The end is near, find a place
to huddle down and pray.

A fox runs over the surveyed
ground. Blessed are the meek

for they shall inherit the Earth.
Blessed the carpenter bee,

the caterpillar and the serpent.
Blessed are those with horns—

cattle, deer, the numbered
buffalo, hallowed be thy name.

Blessed the pitchforks
that lift up the hay.

Blessed the trees now marked
with X's. Body of Christ, full

of grace, cowslip and May
apple. Gone the wake-robin,

Indian pipe, ginseng, and wood
violet. All turned to dust

and for this—a church
filled with hymnals

from which we will mouth
the words.

Listen, the sound of wings—
geese flying south.

Solitude Flats

In the back of the rusted-out Ford
pickup with the missing tailgate

is a load of cedar posts
recently pulled from the ground.

Still attached are porcelain knobs
used to secure electrical fencing.

You can tell how far down
each post was buried. The earth

forever stained into pliable flesh.
She was only a girl

when her father picked up an axe,
walked to the grove of cedars.

The place where Christmas trees
came from in winter,

where bluebirds returned to nest
in spring. She sings

her morning prayers as she reigns
over a two-lane highway. Glad

to see the fields set free at last.
No cows to tend, no bales of hay

to throw, no more keeping
something in.

Something So Grand

I see them each morning
on my drive into work—

two sisters, aging fairies,
still dressed

in soft night gowns,
half hidden from view

by sunflowers
and roses.

Coffee cups in hand,
they stand

barefoot and oblivious
to the world.

It always makes me
a little sad to think

I'm rushing away
from something so grand.

The Beekeeper's Daughter

—after Shaker Village at Pleasant Hill, Kentucky

I start to protest as you advance
toward a swarm of honeybees.

But it is too late, you are there,
standing in the center.

It does not matter that earthbound
feet cannot lift your human frame.

Already your hands gleam
with bright-winged jewels.

Drowsy and full of honey,
they have made you Queen.

You do not hear me call your name.
The steady murmur, this ancient

purpose, too much a part of you now.
The earth turns too fast beneath us.

I push back the urge to rescue you,
think of summers

when I was a child-God:
the thorn-like

stingers left behind
as offerings.

Killing Time

The old woman in the Dollar Store
buys a child's swimming pool—

a rigid circle
of watery blue plastic.

It could be a surprise
for a grandchild

or a faithful companion
who has never been to a groomer.

Maybe I'm romanticizing
the story. Perhaps

she wants to soak her aching feet.
I watch her cross the parking lot,

blue disc in a palsied hand,
and suddenly I want to follow

her home. Watch her sit
in a sagging lawn chair—

filling up the emptiness.

Mother's Day

Think empty rooms
with framed photos.

Think of a woman
tending a garden—

her windswept
hair a white peony.

Think green
pastures of timothy,

apple trees,
the fading

laughter of children.
Think halo

around the moon,
an eclipse of moths,

the porch light left on.

One Good Life

You knew the way to a steamboat captain's grave
overtaken by briars and poison ivy. Buried

standing up, you said—facing east where a bend
in the river bent prisms of light

across the valley floor. But I was always
too busy and it's only today that I remembered

how you asked me to climb that long hill
with you, and now disease, that stern mercenary,

has laid claim to your blood and your one good
life, and all is too late, and never again.

For today they took your right leg. Cut it off
below the knee. Looking at you, all I can see

is a faraway cliff above a great winding river—
muddy water churning behind your closed eyes.

The Mourners

—for Gertrude (1897–1988)

They entered the room like
a covey of doves, five old

friends who had all buried
husbands. Like flightless

blackbirds, sturdy shoes
turned toward beloved

Gertrude. Behind them,
rows of empty chairs

stood like wooden storks.
Handkerchiefs were pressed

to breasts as if comforting
a newborn. They smelled

of nutmeg and cinnamon,
of sage and coriander,

as if moments before
they slipped off a threadbare

apron, placed it behind
a milk white door.

After the Service

Strangers are walking through your house.
They test the water pressure, go so far

as to flush the commode, poke
around in the attic. They want to know

the age of the roof, how close the nearest
school. In their minds, they knock down

walls to accommodate furniture,
make plans to paint the walls

of your bedroom. Something was said
about ripping out the roses.

So hard to maintain.
These foggy mornings in late summer

promise an early frost.
Already the sunflowers have lost their heads.

Hummingbirds grow restless.

Boy Kings

You've been involuntarily admitted
to the VA hospital, on the seventh

floor, where they lock the door
behind you. It's the fourth of July

weekend. I bring you cigarettes
but secretly wish we could run

all the way back to our childhood,
buy novelty fireworks from Jacobi's

grocery—sparklers in red, white
and blue boxes, Cherry Bombs,

Black Cat firecrackers and Pharaoh's
Snakes—

those charcoal black ash serpents
that writhed and twisted and hissed

when you lit them.
I stood behind you, looked over

your shoulder, watched as you
set fire to each round black cylinder.

Afterwards, we did not slay them,
it was the killing winds that took them.

As the last rays of the setting sun
strike the windowpane, your red

hair is gilded with gold. You smoke
cigarette after cigarette while I think

of desert lands and venomous wars,
of tombs, and boy kings.

Upon the Death of a Poet

Each time a poet dies, the soft
spot on a baby's crown closes.

Silence comes to the fields
and stays

like a fifth season. Colors
fade. Puddles of wings

appear in the corners of rooms.
And we cannot remember

a time when there has been
so much rain. Even the deer

stop coming to the salt block.
They must know

we cannot endure such grace.
Grief sits on a shelf

in our study. We reach for it
when a flutter of butterflies

lifts from the last of the asters.
When a pair of heron

pierce the blue
with their long, lyrical lines.

Praise Be to Crows

Let it be late autumn.
Let there be a small town.

Let it be surrounded by cornfields.
Let there be crows.

Let their numbers be incalculable.
Let neither laser nor cannon send them away.

Let them settle inside the eaves of our houses.
Let them sleep in the tops of our trees.

Let silos spill over with shiny black feathers.
Let the fields grow dark with wings.

Let it be done.
Let the machinery be silenced.

Praise be to crows.

II

Toward the Light

What Holds Us Up

This was once a dark, dangerous attic.
Old tube and knob wiring crisscrossed

worn out insulation. I remember,
we celebrated when the last nail

was driven into the two by ten
floor joists—a fine ribcage

for the second story addition. Tonight,
I lie suspended above that ribcage,

soaking in a claw foot tub. Candlelight
warms the butter-crème walls. When

I close my eyes, I can feel the sting
of blisters earned from hammers swung

those long days of summer. We know
each tile intimately. Kneeled

as we placed each one. Prayers
are hidden throughout this house.

Written in drywall compound, folded
in the shutters we hung in the kitchen.

The tongue
and groove flooring

chants
as we walk to our bedroom.

Inkblot (Married Sleep)

Viewed from overhead,
we form an inkblot

as we lie in bed.
Each facing an outer wall,

backs together, knees
bent in unison, soles

of our feet touching.
We could be a butterfly

or some monster
ready to pounce upon

the unsuspecting other.
The something wed

to symmetry—
mirrored, married sleep.

The Seventh Day

On Saturdays, you pull weeds
from the pea gravel path

that winds through the peonies.
I do laundry, clean the house.

We talk little, except for small
pleasantries:

I made another pot of coffee.
Did you see—

the potted begonia, blooming.
But today we sit together

under a covered porch.
You with your watercolors,

me with my pen.
We suffer together the news

of the death of a friend.
You paint a river of salmon—

life-like and striving.
I write this poem.

Where the Crocus Waits

You dig the peonies.
I replant them. I think about

how much we love this work,
the uprooting, the thinning,

the covering up.
It's our secret work.

Both of us dizzy with visions
of blooms that will come

in another season.
We know what beauty

lies beneath the surface.
What it is to wait.

One day, we too shall know
this splendor—

disappear
to where the crocus waits—

where nothing
matters but the will to flower.

The great pushing up.

A Morning in Spring

Where we live, banks
of the Little Pigeon,

a mute mouth.
My kisses cannot save you.

Your soft eyes,
the cormorant rain.

This is how it feels
to disappear. This

thin air.
There should be dragon

boats rushing downstream.
Lanterns to release—

touchstones
for stolen dreams. Each

waking tree in mourning.

The Reckoning

Every dawn brings a sorrow,
each waking hour a dying,

a trucker too tired to slow down,
murmuration of low wheeling

starlings, all those broken
birds dead on the highway.

This is how it has always been—
a doe lying on the shoulder,

gaping hole where her
stomach had been, in the grass

something hiding,
a sharp-shinned hawk, patient

as a clock, in the crotch
of a Japanese maple.

We turn away from the killing,
the neighbor's cat with a limp

wren in its mouth. We pretend
no one is counting the days

quickening
on a merciful wind.

How to Grieve in Winter

In waiting rooms of intensive care units,
women sit, stand or lie down in front of

strangers. Little warmth, still our bodies
lean toward the light. We search

for nourishment in vending machines,
pace back and forth in narrow hallways,

toss and turn on commercial couches,
sign a durable power of attorney. I want

to run outside, gather firewood, chop
off my hair, stain my face with the husks

of walnuts, leave my handprint on the
wall of a cave, pour a prayer into a sand

painting, make pilgrimage to a sacred
mountain, set fire to a braid of sweet grass.

Then cleanse your body with oil of cedar,
cover us both with the skin of a grizzly.

Sleep straight through this long mean
season. Dream ourselves back to a new

beginning.

Uninhabited Continents

Let me tell you how they cut
the clothes from his body,

how in the end,
each machine-fed thread

slipped away,
how his cotton shirt,

his permanent
press slacks

lay like a tailor's pattern—
the shape of them,

uninhabited continents,
flat

on the laundry room floor—
slab

of limestone sky and water.

Sitting with the Dead

There are no words
for this noble

loneliness.
My tongue

struggles
against the roof

of my mouth.
Swallows

lay bricks
behind my eyes,

my teeth
become tiny chairs.

Adrift

In night dreams,
I reach for you.

The bed a still lake
where a blue

heron wades.
Emptiness

floods the hollow
room

and I drown,
again and again,

in the swimming
dark.

Sunday

I remembered the boxes
placed in the attic

after cleaning out your closet,
your cedar chest-of-drawers.

Socks mated, stacked in pairs.
Hats sitting on the top shelf—

frayed caps, the wide-brimmed
that blocked out the sun.

Musk of your dark hair
still lingers inside them—

that sheltered place
I seldom allow myself to enter.

The smell of earth—
remembering the first time

we turned over the garden.
Mindlessly

filling bird feeders,
catching rain in a barrel.

Late Tomatoes

We were beautiful then—
garden gods

tending red globes of light.
Hands the scent of copper

and grass. But now,
in this single

earthbound life,
in a season of frost

and leaf fall,
the dead are yellow stars—

blooms too late to bear.

On the Anniversary of Your Death

You would have taken a lover by now.
It has something to do with thunder,

with clouds, swell and skirr.
It has something to do with hunger.

The body knows what it wants.
It has something to do with trembling,

with release and resurrection.
It has something to do with rain—

evaporating,
then falling on the other side of the world.

Still Life After Abstinence

After a time, you stop
looking in mirrors, keep

the company of trees,
refuse cream in coffee,

linger
wide-eyed in darkness.

You stop reciting prayers.
Now I lay me.

Everything
becomes a prayer—

sunlit window,
bath towel drying on a chair,

loose threads on the hem
of a favorite dress.

Worn

To the twentysomething
boy who will buy

my late husband's
505 Levi's

at the Goodwill
on Lincoln Avenue,

please remember—
love is as fragile

as a lost bird.
One day you will find

the small hole
in the front pocket,

made by a silver
Zippo inscribed

Loved Beyond Measure.
From that moment on,

each time you slide
the worn bronze zipper,

you will listen for the rain,
thinking about a girl

you have yet to meet
on a street

in a monsoon season,
where you will walk,

side by side, a perfect
fit. Her fledgling

hand in your back pocket.

The Naming

I look out the window
at the frozen pond

and I cannot remember
the word for *cattail*

and I cannot think of it
no matter how long

I stare. I begin the naming.
I say out loud—

mockingbird, mailbox,
sky. But the word

that matters is caught
somewhere

in the haze of my breath
on the cold gray glass,

where I trace with a fingertip
letters of the alphabet,

and I say out loud—
drumstick beaters,

because of their shape,
and I say—

a nesting material for birds,
as a clutch of sallow seeds

escape those ragged dark
brown heads.

Parting the Crows

A murder of crows
crowd the cold highway,

take flight
seconds before the car

parts them
and they evaporate,

black wings
oaring in the wind.

I feel it in my heart.
This rush of wings,

a vacuum sound,
like swimming under water.

That first shining surprise
as I rise

through the placid surface,
harvesting air.

Made Beautiful

I'll tell you how I survived
losing you. I dug up

the backyard.
Out came the shrubs.

American barberry,
forsythia, azalea.

I toppled trees.
Dogwood, redbud, sugar

maple. I could not stop,
could not spare

even one perennial.
Peony. Bearded iris.

No bulb survived.
Daffodil, dahlia, calla

lily. Still,
I could not rest until

neither single stem
nor blade remained.

Starlings,
preening flight feathers,

watched from the crest
of a neighbor's

black locust tree.
Alone, brooding

over cups of tepid tea,
I waited patiently

for the return of the fireflies.
Only then could I burn

the clothes
they cut from your body.

Now this land
lies open and fertile.

My hands made beautiful.

The Blue Light of May

It's not for me to say where hours
bleed. Anemic days

filled with one hand-washed cup,
one plate. Friends have stopped

dropping off made-from-scratch
chocolate cakes but our bedroom

still holds our essence
between the folds of satin

drapes. No one told me
how long this sharp-edged road.

I know only one day I woke
and found a faint footpath.

I marvel at the slightest change.
At dawn,

it was a host of robins
rejoicing in the blue light of May.

Tall Grass

In the history of the Great Plains,
women went insane

with *prairie madness*—
the incessant wind,

the never-ending grief of grass.
But I have learned to sleep

in meadows where fireflies
lay eggs then die,

and the wind blows
through the tall grass of my body.

My limbs are made of crowfoot,
backbone foxtail millet.

My hair one long braid of curly dock.
Sedge grass takes root in the marrow

of my bones, and my breasts
weep with the sap of milkweed.

On the day the earth takes me back,
my spirit will rise like the wild

cane that grows
on the banks of a narrow stream.

About the Author

Jessica D. Thompson, a native of Kentucky, lives in a stone house on twenty-five acres at the edge of a classified forest in Southern Indiana. Most of the poems in *Daybreak and Deep* were written in the nearby village of New Harmony, Indiana, the site of an early Utopian settlement.

For many years, Jessica worked as a Human Resource professional while simultaneously serving as a crisis office volunteer, as well as a hospital and legal advocate for a battered women's shelter.

Her poetry has been nominated for a Pushcart Prize and has been published in numerous journals and anthologies, among them: *Appalachian Heritage, The Southern Review, Ruminate Magazine, Tiferet Journal,* and *Circe's Lament: Anthology of Wild Women Poetry* (Accents Publishing). Her awards include the James Baker Hall Memorial Prize in Poetry (*New Southerner,* 2013) and the Kudzu Poetry Prize (2014). She was a finalist in the Joy Bale Boone Poetry Prize (*The Heartland Review,* 2012), the Janet B. McCabe Poetry Prize (*Ruminate Magazine,* 2014), and the Betty Gabehart Prize in Poetry (Kentucky Women Writers, 2016). In 2022, the title poem in this collection, "Daybreak and Deep," was a finalist in the Joy Bale Boone Poetry Prize (*The Heartland Review*).

She has a soft spot for dogs, butter croissants, and strong, black coffee.